PORSCHE 911

60 YEARS OF HISTORY IN PICTURES

FERNANDO MARTÍNEZ

CLASSIC CARS FOREVER

PORSCHE 911

60 YEARS OF HISTORY

IN PICTURES

BOOKS IN THIS SERIES
"CLASSIC CARS FOREVER"

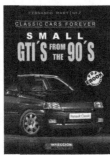

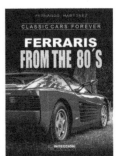

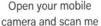

Open your mobile
camera and scan me

OTHER SERIES

"HISTORY OF FORMULA 1"

"COLORING BOOKS"

CONTENTS

911 F

1963-1973

911 (F) 2.0
(1965)

ENGINE: 6-cylinder boxer 2,0 - 130 HP. **MAXIMUM TORQUE:** 174 Nm @ 4,200 rpm. **TOP SPEED:** 210 km/h. **ACCELERATION 0-100 KM/H:** 9.0 sec. **AVERAGE FUEL CONSUMPTION:** 14.5 l/100 km. **DIMENSIONS (length/width/height):** 4.16 x 1.61 x 1.32 m. **WHEELBASE:** 2.21 m. **TYRES:** 165 HR 15. **WEIGHT:** 1,080 kg. **ON SALE:** 1965 - 1968. VALUE IN 2025: 150,000 - 200,000 eur.

911 (F) L
(1968)

ENGINE: 6-cylinder boxer 2,0 - **130 HP**. **MAXIMUM TORQUE:** 174 Nm @ 4,200 rpm. **TOP SPEED:** 210 km/h. **ACCELERATION 0-100 KM/H:** 9.0 sec. **AVERAGE FUEL CONSUMPTION:** 14.5 l/100 km. **DIMENSIONS (length/width/height):** 4.16 x 1.61 x 1.32 m. **WHEELBASE:** 2.21 m. **TYRES:** 165 HR 15. **WEIGHT:** 1,080 kg. **ON SALE:** 1968. **VALUE IN 2025:** 60,000 - 90,000 eur.

911 (F) T
(1968)

ENGINE: 6-cylinder boxer 2,0 - 110 HP. **MAXIMUM TORQUE:** 157 Nm @ 4,200 rpm. **TOP SPEED:** 200 km/h. **ACCELERATION 0-100 KM/H:** 10.0 sec. **AVERAGE FUEL CONSUMPTION:** 14.5 l/100 km. **DIMENSIONS (length/ width/height):** 4.16 x 1.61 x 1.32 m. **WHEELBASE:** 2.26 m. **TYRES:** 165 HR 15. **WEIGHT:** 1,080 kg. **ON SALE:** 1968 - 1969. **VALUE IN 2025:** 80,000 - 100,000 eur.

911 (F) T 2.2
(1970)

ENGINE: 6-cylinder boxer 2,2 - **125 HP**. **MAXIMUM TORQUE:** 176 Nm @ 4,200 rpm. **TOP SPEED:** 205 km/h. **ACCELERATION 0-100 KM/H:** 10.0 sec. **AVERAGE FUEL CONSUMPTION:** 14.5 l/100 km. **DIMENSIONS (length/width/height):** 4.16 x 1.61 x 1.32 m. **WHEELBASE:** 2.26 m. **TYRES:** 165 HR 15. **WEIGHT:** 1,110 kg. **ON SALE:** 1970 - 1971. **VALUE IN 2025:** 80,000 - 100,000 eur.

911 (F) E 2.2
(1970)

ENGINE: 6-cylinder boxer 2,2 - **155 HP**. **MAXIMUM TORQUE:** 191 Nm @ 4,500 rpm. **TOP SPEED:** 215 km/h. **ACCELERATION 0-100 KM/H:** 9.0 sec. **AVERAGE FUEL CONSUMPTION:** 15.5 l/100 km. **DIMENSIONS (length/width/height):** 4.16 x 1.61 x 1.32 m. **WHEELBASE:** 2.26 m. **TYRES:** 185/70 VR 15. **WEIGHT:** 1,110 kg. **ON SALE:** 1970 - 1971. VALUE IN 2025: 80,000 - 100,000 eur.

911 (F) S 2.4
[1972]

ENGINE: 6-cylinder boxer 2,4 - 190 HP. **MAXIMUM TORQUE:** 216 Nm @ 5,200 rpm. **TOP SPEED:** 230 km/h. **ACCELERATION 0-100 KM/H:** 7.5 sec. **AVERAGE FUEL CONSUMPTION:** 17.0 l/100 km. **DIMENSIONS (length/width/height):** 4.16 x 1.61 x 1.32 m. **WHEELBASE:** 2.27 m. **TYRES:** 185/70 VR 15. **WEIGHT:** 1,075 kg. **ON SALE:** 1972 - 1973. VALUE IN 2025: 140,000 - 170,000 eur.

911 [F] CARRERA RS 2.7
[1972]

ENGINE: 6-cylinder boxer 2,7 - **210 HP**. **MAXIMUM TORQUE:** 255 Nm @ 5,100 rpm. **TOP SPEED:** 245 km/h. **ACCELERATION 0-100 KM/H:** 5.8 sec. **AVERAGE FUEL CONSUMPTION:** 18.0 l/100 km. **DIMENSIONS (length/width/height):** 4.16 x 1.65 x 1.32 m. **WHEELBASE:** 2.27 m. **TYRES:** 185/70 VR 15 (front) - 215/60 VR 15 (rear). **WEIGHT:** 975 kg. **ON SALE:** 1972. **VALUE IN 2025:** 100,000 - 240,000 eur.

911 G

1973-1989

911 (G)
(1973)

ENGINE: 6-cylinder boxer 2,7 - 190 HP. **MAXIMUM TORQUE:** 235 Nm @ 3,800 rpm. **TOP SPEED:** 210 km/h. **ACCELERATION 0-100 KM/H:** 8.5 sec. **AVERAGE FUEL CONSUMPTION:** 14.0 l/100 km. **DIMENSIONS (length/width/height):** 4.29 x 1.61 x 1.32 m. **WHEELBASE:** 2.27 m. **TYRES:** 165 HR15. **WEIGHT:** 1,075 kg. **ON SALE:** 1973 - 1975. VALUE IN 2025: 40,000 - 60,000 eur.

911 [G]
[1975]

ENGINE: 6-cylinder boxer 2,7 - **165 HP**. **MAXIMUM TORQUE:** 235 Nm @ 4,000 rpm. **TOP SPEED:** 215 km/h. **ACCELERATION 0-100 KM/H:** 7.8 sec. **AVERAGE FUEL CONSUMPTION:** 15.0 l/100 km. **DIMENSIONS (length/width/height):** 4.29 x 1.61 x 1.32 m. **WHEELBASE:** 2.27 m. **TYRES:** 185/70VR 15. **WEIGHT:** 1,120 kg. **ON SALE:** 1975 - 1978. VALUE IN 2025: 50,000 - 70,000 eur.

911 [G] CARRERA 3.0
[1975]

ENGINE: 6-cylinder boxer 3,0 - **200 HP**. **MAXIMUM TORQUE:** 255 Nm @ 4,200 rpm. **TOP SPEED:** 235 km/h. **ACCELERATION 0-100 KM/H:** 6.5 sec. **AVERAGE FUEL CONSUMPTION:** 17.0 l/100 km. **DIMENSIONS (length/width/height):** 4.29 x 1.65 x 1.32 m. **WHEELBASE:** 2.27 m. **TYRES:** 185/70 VR 15 (front) - 215/60 VR 15 (rear). **WEIGHT:** 1,120 kg. **ON SALE:** 1975 - 1977. **VALUE IN 2025:** 80,000 - 100,000 eur.

LY 86705

911 (930) TURBO 3.0
(1974)

ENGINE: 6-cylinder boxer 3,0 turbo - **260 HP**. **MAXIMUM TORQUE:** 343 Nm @ 4,000 rpm. **TOP SPEED:** 250 km/h. **ACCELERATION 0-100 KM/H:** 5.5 sec. **AVERAGE FUEL CONSUMPTION:** 20.0 l/100 km. **DIMENSIONS (length/width/height):** 4.29 x 1.77 x 1.32 m. **WHEELBASE:** 2.27 m. **TYRES:** 205/55 VR 16 (front) - 225/50 VR 16 (rear). **WEIGHT:** 1,195 kg. **ON SALE:** 1974 - 1977. VALUE IN 2025: 80,000 - 180,000 eur.

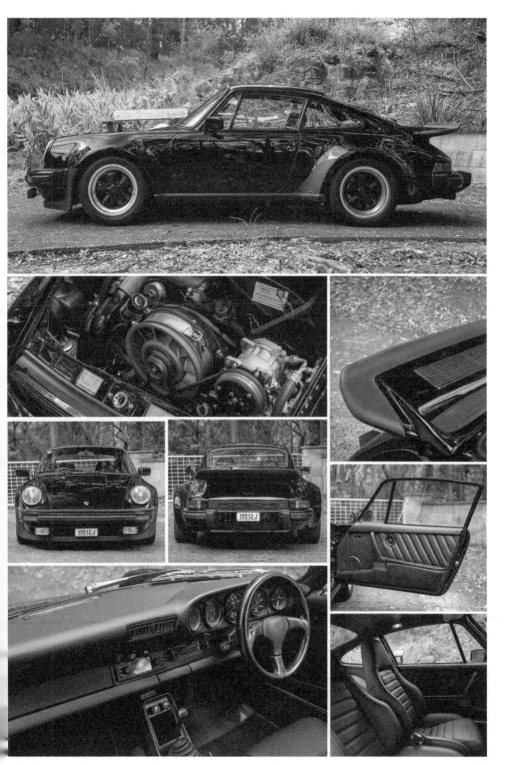

911 (930) TURBO 3.3
(1978)

ENGINE: 6-cylinder boxer 3,3 turbo - **300 HP**. **MAXIMUM TORQUE:** 430 Nm @ 4,000 rpm. **TOP SPEED:** 260 km/h. **ACCELERATION 0-100 KM/H:** 5.2 sec. **AVERAGE FUEL CONSUMPTION:** 20.0 l/100 km. **DIMENSIONS (length/width/height):** 4.29 x 1.77 x 1.32 m. **WHEELBASE:** 2.27 m. **TYRES:** 205/55 VR 16 (front) - 245/45 VR 16 (rear). **WEIGHT:** 1,335 kg. **ON SALE:** 1978 - 1989. **VALUE IN 2025:** 80,000 - 250,000 eur.

911 (G) SC
(1980)

ENGINE: 6-cylinder boxer 3,0 - **204 HP**. **MAXIMUM TORQUE:** 267 Nm @ 4,300 rpm. **TOP SPEED:** 235 km/h. **ACCELERATION 0-100 KM/H:** 6.5 sec. **AVERAGE FUEL CONSUMPTION:** 15.5 l/100 km. **DIMENSIONS (length/width/height):** 4.29 x 1.65 x 1.32 m. **WHEELBASE:** 2.27 m. **TYRES:** 185/70 VR 15 (front) - 215/60 VR 15 (rear). **WEIGHT:** 1,180 kg. **ON SALE:** 1980 - 1983. **VALUE IN 2025:** 40,000 - 50,000 eur.

911 [G] CARRERA 3.2
[1984]

ENGINE: 6-cylinder boxer 3,2 - **231 HP**. **MAXIMUM TORQUE:** 284 Nm @ 4,800 rpm. **TOP SPEED:** 245 km/h. **ACCELERATION 0-100 KM/H:** 6.1 sec. **AVERAGE FUEL CONSUMPTION:** 15.0 l/100 km. **DIMENSIONS (length/width/height):** 4.29 x 1.65 x 1.32 m. **WHEELBASE:** 2.27 m. **TYRES:** 195/65 ZR 15 (front) - 215/60 ZR 15 (rear). **WEIGHT:** 1,210 kg. **ON SALE:** 1984 - 1989. **VALUE IN 2025:** 60,000 - 80,000 eur.

911 (G) SPEEDSTER
(1989)

ENGINE: 6-cylinder boxer 3,2 - **231 HP**. **MAXIMUM TORQUE:** 284 Nm @ 4,800 rpm. **TOP SPEED:** 245 km/h. **ACCELERATION 0-100 KM/H:** 6.0 sec. **AVERAGE FUEL CONSUMPTION:** 14.0 l/100 km. **DIMENSIONS (length/width/height):** 4.29 x 1.77 x 1.28 m. **WHEELBASE:** 2.27 m. **TYRES:** 205/55 ZR 16 (front) - 255/45 ZR 16 (rear). **WEIGHT:** 1,350 kg. **ON SALE:** 1989. **VALUE IN 2025:** 180,000 - 220,000 eur.

911 (964)

1988-1994

911 [964] CARRERA 2
[1989]

ENGINE: 6-cylinder boxer 3,6 - **250 HP**. **MAXIMUM TORQUE:** 310 Nm @ 4,800 rpm. **TOP SPEED:** 260 km/h. **ACCELERATION 0-100 KM/H:** 5.7 sec. **AVERAGE FUEL CONSUMPTION:** 14.0 l/100 km. **DIMENSIONS (length/width/height):** 4.25 x 1.65 x 1.31 m. **WHEELBASE:** 2.27 m. **TYRES:** 205/55 ZR 16 (front) - 225/50 ZR 16 (rear). **WEIGHT:** 1,350 kg. **ON SALE:** 1989 - 1994. **VALUE IN 2025:** 60,000 - 120,000 eur.

911 [964] CARRERA 4
[1989]

ENGINE: 6-cylinder boxer 3,6 - **250 HP**. **MAXIMUM TORQUE:** 310 Nm @ 4,800 rpm. **TOP SPEED:** 260 km/h. **ACCELERATION 0-100 KM/H:** 5.7 sec. **AVERAGE FUEL CONSUMPTION:** 14.0 l/100 km. **DIMENSIONS (length/width/height):** 4.25 x 1.65 x 1.31 m. **WHEELBASE:** 2.27 m. **TYRES:** 205/55 ZR 16 (front) - 225/50 ZR 16 (rear). **WEIGHT:** 1,450 kg. **ON SALE:** 1989 - 1994. **VALUE IN 2025:** 60,000 - 120,000 eur.

911 (964) TURBO 3.3
(1990)

ENGINE: 6-cylinder boxer 3,3 - **320 HP**. **MAXIMUM TORQUE:** 450 Nm @ 4,400 rpm. **TOP SPEED:** 270 km/h. **ACCELERATION 0-100 KM/H:** 5.0 sec. **AVERAGE FUEL CONSUMPTION:** 22.8 l/100 km. **DIMENSIONS (length/width/height):** 4.25 x 1.77 x 1.31 m. **WHEELBASE:** 2.27 m. **TYRES:** 205/50 ZR 17 (front) - 255/40 ZR 17 (rear). **WEIGHT:** 1,470 kg. **ON SALE:** 1990 - 1993. **VALUE IN 2025:** 80,000 - 200,000 eur.

911 [964] CARRERA RS
[1992]

ENGINE: 6-cylinder boxer 3,6 - 260 HP. **MAXIMUM TORQUE:** 325 Nm @ 4,800 rpm. **TOP SPEED:** 260 km/h. **ACCELERATION 0-100 KM/H:** 5.3 sec. **AVERAGE FUEL CONSUMPTION:** 15.0 l/100 km. **DIMENSIONS (length/width/height):** 4.25 x 1.65 x 1.31 m. **WHEELBASE:** 2.27 m. **TYRES:** 205/50 ZR 17 (front) - 255/40 ZR 17 (rear). **WEIGHT:** 1,220 kg. **ON SALE:** 1992. **VALUE IN 2025:** 150,000 - 250,000 eur.

911 (964) TURBO S
(1992)

ENGINE: 6-cylinder boxer 3,3 - **381 HP**. **MAXIMUM TORQUE:** 490 Nm @ 4,800 rpm. **TOP SPEED:** 290 km/h. **ACCELERATION 0-100 KM/H:** 4.7 sec. **AVERAGE FUEL CONSUMPTION:** 15.0 l/100 km. **DIMENSIONS (length/width/height):** 4.27 x 1.77 x 1.27 m. **WHEELBASE:** 2.27 m. **TYRES:** 225/40 ZR 18 (front) - 265/35 ZR 18 (rear). **WEIGHT:** 1,290 kg. **ON SALE:** 1992. **VALUE IN 2025:** 100,000 - 220,000 eur.

911 [964] TURBO 3.6
[1993]

ENGINE: 6-cylinder boxer 3,6 - **360 HP**. **MAXIMUM TORQUE:** 520 Nm @ 4,200 rpm. **TOP SPEED:** 280 km/h. **ACCELERATION 0-100 KM/H:** 4.8 sec. **AVERAGE FUEL CONSUMPTION:** 18.0 l/100 km. **DIMENSIONS (length/width/height):** 4.25 x 1.77 x 1.31 m. **WHEELBASE:** 2.27 m. **TYRES:** 225/40 ZR 18 (front) - 265/35 ZR 18 (rear). **WEIGHT:** 1,470 kg. **ON SALE:** 1993 - 1994. **VALUE IN 2025:** 80,000 - 200,000 eur.

911 [964] CARRERA RS 3.8
[1993]

ENGINE: 6-cylinder boxer 3,8 - 300 HP. **MAXIMUM TORQUE:** 360 Nm @ 5,250 rpm. **TOP SPEED:** 271 km/h. **ACCELERATION 0-100 KM/H:** 5.2 sec. **AVERAGE FUEL CONSUMPTION:** 15.3 l/100 km. **DIMENSIONS (length/width/height):** 4.27 x 1.77 x 1.27 m. **WHEELBASE:** 2.27 m. **TYRES:** 225/40 ZR 18 (front) - 265/35 ZR 18 (rear). **WEIGHT:** 1,249 kg. **ON SALE:** 1993. **VALUE IN 2025:** 200,000 - 230,000 eur.

911 [993]

1993-1998

911 [993] CARRERA 2
[1993]

ENGINE: 6-cylinder boxer 3,6 - **270 HP**. **MAXIMUM TORQUE:** 330 Nm @ 5,000 rpm. **TOP SPEED:** 270 km/h. **ACCELERATION 0-100 KM/H:** 5.6 sec. **AVERAGE FUEL CONSUMPTION:** 11.4 l/100 km. **DIMENSIONS (length/width/height):** 4.24 x 1.73 x 1.31 m. **WHEELBASE:** 2.27 m. **TYRES:** 205/50 ZR 17 (front) - 255/40 ZR 17 (rear). **WEIGHT:** 1,370 kg. **ON SALE:** 1993 - 1998. **VALUE IN 2025:** 60,000 - 100,000 eur.

911 [993] CARRERA 4
[1993]

ENGINE: 6-cylinder boxer 3,6 - 270 HP. **MAXIMUM TORQUE:** 330 Nm @ 5,000 rpm. **TOP SPEED:** 270 km/h. **ACCELERATION 0-100 KM/H:** 5.4 sec. **AVERAGE FUEL CONSUMPTION:** 11.5 l/100 km. **DIMENSIONS (length/width/height):** 4.24 x 1.73 x 1.31 m. **WHEELBASE:** 2.27 m. **TYRES:** 205/50 ZR 17 (front) - 255/40 ZR 17 (rear). **WEIGHT:** 1,420 kg. **ON SALE:** 1993 - 1998. **VALUE IN 2025:** 60,000 - 100,000 eur.

67

911 [993] CARRERA RS
[1993]

ENGINE: 6-cylinder boxer 3,8 - **300 HP**. **MAXIMUM TORQUE:** 355 Nm @ 5,400 rpm. **TOP SPEED:** 277 km/h. **ACCELERATION 0-100 KM/H:** 5.0 sec. **AVERAGE FUEL CONSUMPTION:** 12.4 l/100 km. **DIMENSIONS (length/width/height):** 4.24 x 1.73 x 1.31 m. **WHEELBASE:** 2.27 m. **TYRES:** 225/40 ZR 18 (front) - 265/35 ZR 18 (rear). **WEIGHT:** 1,270 kg. **ON SALE:** 1993. **VALUE IN 2025:** 150,000 - 400,000 eur.

911 (993) TURBO
(1995)

ENGINE: 6-cylinder boxer 3,6 - 408 HP. **MAXIMUM TORQUE:** 540 Nm @ 4,500 rpm. **TOP SPEED:** 290 km/h. **ACCELERATION 0-100 KM/H:** 4.5 sec. **AVERAGE FUEL CONSUMPTION:** 13.2 l/100 km. **DIMENSIONS (length/width/height):** 4.24 x 1.79 x 1.31 m. **WHEELBASE:** 2.27 m. **TYRES:** 225/40 ZR 18 (front) - 285/30 ZR 18 (rear). **WEIGHT:** 1,500 kg. **ON SALE:** 1995 - 1998. **VALUE IN 2025:** 100,000 - 300,000 eur.

911 [993] CARRERA S
[1997]

ENGINE: 6-cylinder boxer 3,6 - **286 HP**. **MAXIMUM TORQUE:** 340 Nm @ 5,250 rpm. **TOP SPEED:** 270 km/h. **ACCELERATION 0-100 KM/H:** 5.3 sec. **AVERAGE FUEL CONSUMPTION:** 11.5 l/100 km. **DIMENSIONS (length/width/height):** 4.24 x 1.79 x 1.31 m. **WHEELBASE:** 2.27 m. **TYRES:** 225/40 ZR 18 (front) - 285/30 ZR 18 (rear). **WEIGHT:** 1,400 kg. **ON SALE:** 1997 - 1998. **VALUE IN 2025:** 80,000 - 140,000 eur.

911 (993) CARRERA 4S
(1996)

ENGINE: 6-cylinder boxer 3,6 - **286 HP**. **MAXIMUM TORQUE:** 340 Nm @ 5,250 rpm. **TOP SPEED:** 270 km/h. **ACCELERATION 0-100 KM/H:** 5.3 sec. **AVERAGE FUEL CONSUMPTION:** 11.5 l/100 km. **DIMENSIONS (length/width/height):** 4.24 x 1.79 x 1.31 m. **WHEELBASE:** 2.27 m. **TYRES:** 225/40 ZR 18 (front) - 285/30 ZR 18 (rear). **WEIGHT:** 1,450 kg. **ON SALE:** 1996 - 1998. **VALUE IN 2025:** 90,000 - 180,000 eur.

911 (993) GT2
(1996)

ENGINE: 6-cylinder boxer 3,6 - **430 HP**. **MAXIMUM TORQUE:** 540 Nm @ 5,750 rpm. **TOP SPEED:** 295 km/h. **ACCELERATION 0-100 KM/H:** 4.4 sec. **AVERAGE FUEL CONSUMPTION:** -- l/100 km. **DIMENSIONS (length/width/height):** 4.24 x 1.85 x 1.31 m. **WHEELBASE:** 2.27 m. **TYRES:** 235/40 ZR 18 (front) - 285/35 ZR 18 (rear). **WEIGHT:** 1,295 kg. **ON SALE:** 1996 - 1998. **VALUE IN 2025:** 500,000 - 1,000,000 eur.

911 [993] TURBO S
[1997]

ENGINE: 6-cylinder boxer 3,6 - 450 HP. **MAXIMUM TORQUE:** 585 Nm @ 4,500 rpm. **TOP SPEED:** 300 km/h. **ACCELERATION 0-100 KM/H:** 4.1 sec. **AVERAGE FUEL CONSUMPTION:** 14.2 l/100 km. **DIMENSIONS (length/width/height):** 4.24 x 1.79 x 1.28 m. **WHEELBASE:** 2.27 m. **TYRES:** 225/40 ZR 18 (front) - 285/30 ZR 18 (rear). **WEIGHT:** 1,500 kg. **ON SALE:** 1997 - 1998. **VALUE IN 2025:** 200,000 - 350,000 eur.

911 (996)

1997-2006

911 (996) CARRERA 2
(1998)

ENGINE: 6-cylinder boxer 3,4 - **300 HP**. **MAXIMUM TORQUE:** 350 Nm @ 4,600 rpm. **TOP SPEED:** 280 km/h. **ACCELERATION 0-100 KM/H:** 5.2 sec. **AVERAGE FUEL CONSUMPTION:** 11.8 l/100 km. **DIMENSIONS (length/width/height):** 4.43 x 1.76 x 1.29 m. **WHEELBASE:** 2.35 m. **TYRES:** 205/50 ZR 17 (front) - 255/40 ZR 17 (rear). **WEIGHT:** 1,320 kg. **ON SALE:** 1998 - 2003. **VALUE IN 2025:** 20,000 - 50,000 eur.

911 [996] CARRERA 4
[1998]

ENGINE: 6-cylinder boxer 3,6 - **300 HP**. **MAXIMUM TORQUE:** 350 Nm @ 4,600 rpm. **TOP SPEED:** 280 km/h. **ACCELERATION 0-100 KM/H:** 5.2 sec. **AVERAGE FUEL CONSUMPTION:** 12.0 l/100 km. **DIMENSIONS (length/width/height):** 4.43 x 1.76 x 1.29 m. **WHEELBASE:** 2.35 m. **TYRES:** 205/50 ZR 17 (front) - 255/40 ZR 17 (rear). **WEIGHT:** 1,375 kg. **ON SALE:** 1998 - 2004. **VALUE IN 2025:** 20,000 - 60,000 eur.

911 [996] CARRERA 4S
[2002]

ENGINE: 6-cylinder boxer 3,6 - **320 HP**. **MAXIMUM TORQUE:** 370 Nm @ 4,250 rpm. **TOP SPEED:** 280 km/h. **ACCELERATION 0-100 KM/H:** 5.1 sec. **AVERAGE FUEL CONSUMPTION:** 11.4 l/100 km. **DIMENSIONS (length/width/height):** 4.43 x 1.83 x 1.29 m. **WHEELBASE:** 2.35 m. **TYRES:** 225/40 ZR 18 (front) - 295/30 ZR 18 (rear). **WEIGHT:** 1,495 kg. **ON SALE:** 2002 - 2004. **VALUE IN 2025:** 35,000 - 70,000 eur.

911 (996) TURBO
(2001)

ENGINE: 6-cylinder boxer 3,6 - **420 HP**. **MAXIMUM TORQUE:** 560 Nm @ 4,600 rpm. **TOP SPEED:** 305 km/h. **ACCELERATION 0-100 KM/H:** 4.2 sec. **AVERAGE FUEL CONSUMPTION:** 12.9 l/100 km. **DIMENSIONS (length/width/height):** 4.43 x 1.83 x 1.29 m. **WHEELBASE:** 2.35 m. **TYRES:** 225/40 ZR 18 (front) - 295/30 ZR 18 (rear). **WEIGHT:** 1,540 kg. **ON SALE:** 2001 - 2006. **VALUE IN 2025:** 50,000 - 100,000 eur.

911 (996) TURBO S
(2004)

ENGINE: 6-cylinder boxer 3,6 - **450 HP**. **MAXIMUM TORQUE:**
620 Nm @ 3,500 rpm. **TOP SPEED:** 307 km/h. **ACCELERATION 0-100 KM/H:**
4.2 sec. **AVERAGE FUEL CONSUMPTION:** 13.3 l/100 km. **DIMENSIONS
(length/width/height):** 4.43 x 1.83 x 1.29 m. **WHEELBASE:** 2.35 m. **TYRES:**
225/40 ZR 18 (front) - 295/30 ZR 18 (rear). **WEIGHT:** 1,540 kg. **ON SALE:** 2004
- 2005. **VALUE IN 2025:** 70,000 - 130,000 eur.

911 (996) GT2 CLUBSPORT
(2001)

ENGINE: 6-cylinder boxer 3,6 - 462 HP. **MAXIMUM TORQUE:** 620 Nm @ 3,500 rpm. **TOP SPEED:** 315 km/h. **ACCELERATION 0-100 KM/H:** 4.1 sec. **AVERAGE FUEL CONSUMPTION:** 12.9 l/100 km. **DIMENSIONS (length/width/height):** 4.45 x 1.83 x 1.29 m. **WHEELBASE:** 2.35 m. **TYRES:** 235/40 ZR 18 (front) - 315/30 ZR 18 (rear). **WEIGHT:** 1,420 kg. **ON SALE:** 2001 - 2005. **VALUE IN 2025:** 200,000 - 250,000 eur.

93

911 [996] GT3
[1999]

ENGINE: 6-cylinder boxer 3,6 - **360 HP**. **MAXIMUM TORQUE:** 370 Nm @ 5,000 rpm. **TOP SPEED:** 302 km/h. **ACCELERATION 0-100 KM/H:** 4.8 sec. **AVERAGE FUEL CONSUMPTION:** 12.9 l/100 km. **DIMENSIONS (length/width/height):** 4.43 x 1.76 x 1.31 m. **WHEELBASE:** 2.35 m. **TYRES:** 225/40 ZR 18 (front) - 285/30 ZR 18 (rear). **WEIGHT:** 1,350 kg. **ON SALE:** 1999 - 2004. **VALUE IN 2025:** 40,000 - 120,000 eur.

911 (996) GT3 RS
(2003)

ENGINE: 6-cylinder boxer 3,6 - **381 HP**. **MAXIMUM TORQUE:** 385 Nm @ 5,000 rpm. **TOP SPEED:** 306 km/h. **ACCELERATION 0-100 KM/H:** 4.3 sec. **AVERAGE FUEL CONSUMPTION:** 12.9 l/100 km. **DIMENSIONS (length/width/height):** 4.43 x 1.77 x 1.31 m. **WHEELBASE:** 2.35 m. **TYRES:** 225/40 ZR 18 (front) - 285/30 ZR 18 (rear). **WEIGHT:** 1,360 kg. **ON SALE:** 2003 - 2005. **VALUE IN 2025:** 200,000 - 250,000 eur.

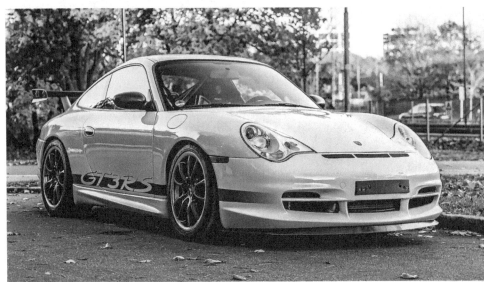

911 (997)

BB · EM 962

2004-2012

911 [997] CARRERA
[2004]

ENGINE: 6-cylinder boxer 3,6 - **325 HP**. **MAXIMUM TORQUE:** 370 Nm @ 4,250 rpm. **TOP SPEED:** 285 km/h. **ACCELERATION 0-100 KM/H:** 5.0 sec. **AVERAGE FUEL CONSUMPTION:** 11.0 l/100 km. **DIMENSIONS (length/width/height):** 4.43 x 1.80 x 1.31 m. **WHEELBASE:** 2.35 m. **TYRES:** 235/40 ZR 18 (front) - 265/40 ZR 18 (rear). **WEIGHT:** 1,490 kg. **ON SALE:** 2004 - 2011. **VALUE IN 2025:** 30,000 - 60,000 eur.

911 [997] CARRERA 4S
[2005]

ENGINE: 6-cylinder boxer 3,8 - **355 HP**. **MAXIMUM TORQUE:** 415 Nm @ 5,500 rpm. **TOP SPEED:** 288 km/h. **ACCELERATION 0-100 KM/H:** 4.8 sec. **AVERAGE FUEL CONSUMPTION:** 11.8 l/100 km. **DIMENSIONS (length/width/height):** 4.43 x 1.85 x 1.30 m. **WHEELBASE:** 2,35 m. **TYRES:** 235/35 ZR 19 (front) - 305/30 ZR 19 (rear). **WEIGHT:** 1,555 kg. **ON SALE:** 2005 - 2012. **VALUE IN 2025:** 40,000 - 70,000 eur.

911 [997] CARRERA GTS
[2012]

ENGINE: 6-cylinder boxer 3,8 - 408 HP. **MAXIMUM TORQUE:** 420 Nm @ 4,200 rpm. **TOP SPEED:** 306 km/h. **ACCELERATION 0-100 KM/H:** 4.6 sec. **AVERAGE FUEL CONSUMPTION:** 10.6 l/100 km. **DIMENSIONS (length/width/height):** 4.43 x 1.85 x 1.30 m. **WHEELBASE:** 2.35 m. **TYRES:** 235/35 ZR 19 (front) - 305/30 ZR 19 (rear). **WEIGHT:** 1,495 kg. **ON SALE:** 2012 - 2014. **VALUE IN 2025:** 70,000 - 130,000 eur.

911 [997] TURBO
[2005]

ENGINE: 6-cylinder boxer 3,6 - 480 HP. **MAXIMUM TORQUE:** 600 Nm @ 4,000 rpm. **TOP SPEED:** 310 km/h. **ACCELERATION 0-100 KM/H:** 3.9 sec. **AVERAGE FUEL CONSUMPTION:** 12.8 l/100 km. **DIMENSIONS (length/width/height):** 4.45 x 1.85 x 1.30 m. **WHEELBASE:** 2.35 m. **TYRES:** 235/35 ZR 19 (front) - 305/30 ZR 19 (rear). **WEIGHT:** 1,645 kg. **ON SALE:** 2005 - 2012. **VALUE IN 2025:** 60,000 - 110,000 eur.

911 [997] TURBO S
[2010]

ENGINE: 6-cylinder boxer 3,8 - **530 HP**. **MAXIMUM TORQUE:** 700 Nm @ 4,250 rpm. **TOP SPEED:** 315 km/h. **ACCELERATION 0-100 KM/H:** 3.5 sec. **AVERAGE FUEL CONSUMPTION:** 11.4 l/100 km. **DIMENSIONS (length/width/height):** 4.45 x 1.85 x 1.30 m. **WHEELBASE:** 2.35 m. **TYRES:** 235/35 ZR 19 (front) - 305/30 ZR 19 (rear). **WEIGHT:** 1,660 kg. **ON SALE:** 2010 - 2012. **VALUE IN 2025:** 85,000 - 200,000 eur.

911 [997] GT3
[2005]

ENGINE: 6-cylinder boxer 3,8 - 435 HP. **MAXIMUM TORQUE:** 430 Nm @ 6,250 rpm. **TOP SPEED:** 312 km/h. **ACCELERATION 0-100 KM/H:** 4.1 sec. **AVERAGE FUEL CONSUMPTION:** 12.8 l/100 km. **DIMENSIONS (length/width/height):** 4.46 x 1.80 x 1.28 m. **WHEELBASE:** 2.35 m. **TYRES:** 235/35 ZR 19 (front) - 305/30 ZR 19 (rear). **WEIGHT:** 1,470 kg. **ON SALE:** 2005 - 2010. **VALUE IN 2025:** 80,000 - 130,000 eur.

911 [997] GT3 RS
[2011]

ENGINE: 6-cylinder boxer 3,8 - 450 HP. **MAXIMUM TORQUE:** 430 Nm @ 6,750 rpm. **TOP SPEED:** 310 km/h. **ACCELERATION 0-100 KM/H:** 4.0 sec. **AVERAGE FUEL CONSUMPTION:** 13.2 l/100 km. **DIMENSIONS (length/width/height):** 4.46 x 1.85 x 1.28 m. **WHEELBASE:** 2.35 m. **TYRES:** 245/35 ZR 19 (front) - 325/30 ZR 19 (rear). **WEIGHT:** 1,445 kg. **ON SALE:** 2011. **VALUE IN 2025:** 160,000 - 240,000 eur.

911 [997] GT2
[2007]

ENGINE: 6-cylinder boxer 3,8 - 530 HP. **MAXIMUM TORQUE:** 680 Nm @ 4,500 rpm. **TOP SPEED:** 329 km/h. **ACCELERATION 0-100 KM/H:** 3.7 sec. **AVERAGE FUEL CONSUMPTION:** 12.5 l/100 km. **DIMENSIONS (length/width/height):** 4.46 x 1.85 x 1.28 m. **WHEELBASE:** 2.35 m. **TYRES:** 235/35 ZR 19 (front) - 325/30 ZR 19 (rear). **WEIGHT:** 1,445 kg. **ON SALE:** 2007 - 2009. **VALUE IN 2025:** 120,000 - 260,000 eur.

911 [997] GT2 RS
[2010]

ENGINE: 6-cylinder boxer 3,6 - **620 HP**. **MAXIMUM TORQUE:** 700 Nm @ 6,500 rpm. **TOP SPEED:** 330 km/h. **ACCELERATION 0-100 KM/H:** 3.5 sec. **AVERAGE FUEL CONSUMPTION:** 11.9 l/100 km. **DIMENSIONS (length/width/height):** 4.47 x 1.85 x 1.28 m. **WHEELBASE:** 2.35 m. **TYRES:** 245/35 ZR 19 (front) - 325/30 ZR 19 (rear). **WEIGHT:** 1,445 kg. **ON SALE:** 2010 - 2011. **VALUE IN 2025:** 300,000 - 500,000 eur.

911 [997] GT3 RS 4.0
[2011]

ENGINE: 6-cylinder boxer 4,0 - **500 HP**. **MAXIMUM TORQUE:** 460 Nm @ 5,750 rpm. **TOP SPEED:** 310 km/h. **ACCELERATION 0-100 KM/H:** 3.9 sec. **AVERAGE FUEL CONSUMPTION:** 13.8 l/100 km. **DIMENSIONS (length/width/height):** 4.47 x 1.85 x 1.28 m. **WHEELBASE:** 2.35 m. **TYRES:** 245/35 ZR 19 (front) - 325/30 ZR 19 (rear). **WEIGHT:** 1,435 kg. **ON SALE:** 2011. **VALUE IN 2025:** 400,000 - 650,000 eur.

911 (991)

2011-2019

911 [991] CARRERA 4
[2011]

ENGINE: 6-cylinder boxer 3,4 - **350 HP**. **MAXIMUM TORQUE:** 390 Nm @ 5,600 rpm. **TOP SPEED:** 285 km/h. **ACCELERATION 0-100 KM/H:** 4.9 sec. **AVERAGE FUEL CONSUMPTION:** 9.3 l/100 km. **DIMENSIONS (length/width/height):** 4.50 x 1.85 x 1.30 m. **WHEELBASE:** 2.45 m. **TYRES:** 235/40 ZR 19 (front) - 295/35 ZR 19 (rear). **WEIGHT:** 1,505 kg. **ON SALE:** 2011 - 2017. **VALUE IN 2025:** 60,000 - 125,000 eur.

911 [991] CARRERA 4S
[2011]

ENGINE: 6-cylinder boxer 3,8 - **400 HP**. **MAXIMUM TORQUE:** 440 Nm @ 5,600 rpm. **TOP SPEED:** 299 km/h. **ACCELERATION 0-100 KM/H:** 4.5 sec. **AVERAGE FUEL CONSUMPTION:** 9.9 l/100 km. **DIMENSIONS (length/width/height):** 4.50 x 1.85 x 1.29 m. **WHEELBASE:** 2.45 m. **TYRES:** 245/35 ZR 20 (front) - 305/30 ZR 20 (rear). **WEIGHT:** 1,520 kg. **ON SALE:** 2011 - 2017. **VALUE IN 2025:** 75,000 - 140,000 eur.

911 [991] CARRERA 4 GTS [2014]

ENGINE: 6-cylinder boxer 3,0 - **450 HP**. **MAXIMUM TORQUE:** 550 Nm @ 5,000 rpm. **TOP SPEED:** 310 km/h. **ACCELERATION 0-100 KM/H:** 4.0 sec. **AVERAGE FUEL CONSUMPTION:** 9.5 l/100 km. **DIMENSIONS (length/width/height):** 4.52 x 1.85 x 1.28 m. **WHEELBASE:** 2.45 m. **TYRES:** 245/35 ZR 20 (front) - 305/30 ZR 20 (rear). **WEIGHT:** 1,570 kg. **ON SALE:** 2014 - 2018. **VALUE IN 2025:** 100,000 - 160,000 eur.

911 [991] TURBO
[2012]

ENGINE: 6-cylinder boxer 3,8 - **520 HP**. **MAXIMUM TORQUE:** 660 Nm @ 5,000 rpm. **TOP SPEED:** 315 km/h. **ACCELERATION 0-100 KM/H:** 3.4 sec. **AVERAGE FUEL CONSUMPTION:** 9.7 l/100 km. **DIMENSIONS (length/width/height):** 4.50 x 1.88 x 1.29 m. **WHEELBASE:** 2.45 m. **TYRES:** 245/35 ZR 20 (front) - 305/30 ZR 20 (rear). **WEIGHT:** 1,670 kg. **ON SALE:** 2012 - 2018. **VALUE IN 2025:** 100,000 - 220,000 eur.

911 [991] TURBO S
[2014]

ENGINE: 6-cylinder boxer 3,0 - **560 HP**. **MAXIMUM TORQUE:** 700 Nm @ 4,250 rpm. **TOP SPEED:** 318 km/h. **ACCELERATION 0-100 KM/H:** 3.1 sec. **AVERAGE FUEL CONSUMPTION:** 9.7 l/100 km. **DIMENSIONS (length/width/height):** 4.50 x 1.88 x 1.29 m. **WHEELBASE:** 2.45 m. **TYRES:** 245/35 ZR 20 (front) - 305/30 ZR 20 (rear). **WEIGHT:** 1,680 kg. **ON SALE:** 2014 - 2018. **VALUE IN 2025:** 150,000 - 340,000 eur.

911 (991) R
(2016)

ENGINE: 6-cylinder boxer 4,0 - 500 HP. **MAXIMUM TORQUE:** 460 Nm @ 6,250 rpm. **TOP SPEED:** 323 km/h. **ACCELERATION 0-100 KM/H:** 3.8 sec. **AVERAGE FUEL CONSUMPTION:** 13.3 l/100 km. **DIMENSIONS (length/width/height):** 4.53 x 1.85 x 1.27 m. **WHEELBASE:** 2.45 m. **TYRES:** 245/35 ZR 20 (front) - 305/30 ZR 20 (rear). **WEIGHT:** 1,445 kg. **ON SALE:** 2016 - 2017. **VALUE IN 2025:** 300,000 - 400,000 eur.

911 (991) GT3
(2013)

ENGINE: 6-cylinder boxer 3,8 - **475 HP**. **MAXIMUM TORQUE:** 440 Nm @ 6,250 rpm. **TOP SPEED:** 315 km/h. **ACCELERATION 0-100 KM/H:** 3.5 sec. **AVERAGE FUEL CONSUMPTION:** 12.4 l/100 km. **DIMENSIONS (length/width/height):** 4.54 x 1.85 x 1.27 m. **WHEELBASE:** 2.45 m. **TYRES:** 245/35 ZR 20 (front) - 305/30 ZR 20 (rear). **WEIGHT:** 1,505 kg. **ON SALE:** 2013 - 2018. **VALUE IN 2025:** 80,000 - 170,000 eur.

911 (991) GT3 RS
(2015)

ENGINE: 6-cylinder boxer 4,0 - **500 HP**. **MAXIMUM TORQUE:** 460 Nm @ 6,250 rpm. **TOP SPEED:** 310 km/h. **ACCELERATION 0-100 KM/H:** 3.3 sec. **AVERAGE FUEL CONSUMPTION:** 12.7 l/100 km. **DIMENSIONS (length/width/height):** 4.54 x 1.88 x 1.29 m. **WHEELBASE:** 2.45 m. **TYRES:** 265/35 ZR 20 (front) - 325/30 ZR 21 (rear). **WEIGHT:** 1,495 kg. **ON SALE:** 2015 - 2018. **VALUE IN 2025:** 160,000 - 300,000 eur.

911 [991] GT2 RS
[2017]

ENGINE: 6-cylinder boxer 3,8 - **700 HP**. **MAXIMUM TORQUE:** 750 Nm @ 4,500 rpm. **TOP SPEED:** 340 km/h. **ACCELERATION 0-100 KM/H:** 2.8 sec. **AVERAGE FUEL CONSUMPTION:** 11.8 l/100 km. **DIMENSIONS (length/width/height):** 4.55 x 1.88 x 1.29 m. **WHEELBASE:** 2.45 m. **TYRES:** 265/35 ZR 20 (front) - 325/30 ZR 21 (rear). **WEIGHT:** 1,545 kg. **ON SALE:** 2017 - 2018. **VALUE IN 2025:** 300,000 - 600,000 eur.

911 [991] TURBO S EXCLUSIVE [2017]

ENGINE: 6-cylinder boxer 3,8 - 607 HP. **MAXIMUM TORQUE:** 750 Nm @ 4,000 rpm. **TOP SPEED:** 330 km/h. **ACCELERATION 0-100 KM/H:** 2.9 sec. **AVERAGE FUEL CONSUMPTION:** 9.1 l/100 km. **DIMENSIONS (length/width/height):** 4.50 x 1.88 x 1.29 m. **WHEELBASE:** 2.45 m. **TYRES:** 245/35 ZR 20 (front) - 305/30 ZR 20 (rear). **WEIGHT:** 1,675 kg. **ON SALE:** 2017 - 2018. **VALUE IN 2025:** 250,000 - 330,000 eur.

911 (992)

2019-

911 [992] CARRERA S
[2019]

ENGINE: 6-cylinder boxer 3,0 - **450 HP**. **MAXIMUM TORQUE:** 530 Nm @ 5,000 rpm. **TOP SPEED:** 308 km/h. **ACCELERATION 0-100 KM/H:** 3.7 sec. **AVERAGE FUEL CONSUMPTION:** 10.1 l/100 km. **DIMENSIONS (length/width/height):** 4.52 x 1.85 x 1.30 m. **WHEELBASE:** 2.45 m. **TYRES:** 245/35 ZR 20 (front) - 305/30 ZR 21 (rear). **WEIGHT:** 1,555 kg. **ON SALE:** 2019 - . **VALUE IN 2025:** 100,000 - 180,000 eur.

911 (992) CARRERA 4S
(2019)

ENGINE: 6-cylinder boxer 3,0 - **450 HP**. **MAXIMUM TORQUE:** 530 Nm @ 5,000 rpm. **TOP SPEED:** 306 km/h. **ACCELERATION 0-100 KM/H:** 3.6 sec. **AVERAGE FUEL CONSUMPTION:** 10.2 l/100 km. **DIMENSIONS (length/width/height):** 4.52 x 1.85 x 1.30 m. **WHEELBASE:** 2.45 m. **TYRES:** 245/35 ZR 20 (front) - 305/30 ZR 21 (rear). **WEIGHT:** 1,605 kg. **ON SALE:** 2019 - . **VALUE IN 2025:** 100,000 - 190,000 eur.

911 (992) CARRERA GTS
(2021)

ENGINE: 6-cylinder boxer 3,0 - **480 HP**. **MAXIMUM TORQUE:** 570 Nm @ 5,000 rpm. **TOP SPEED:** 311 km/h. **ACCELERATION 0-100 KM/H:** 3.4 sec. **AVERAGE FUEL CONSUMPTION:** 10.4 l/100 km. **DIMENSIONS (length/width/height):** 4.53 x 1.85 x 1.30 m. **WHEELBASE:** 2.45 m. **TYRES:** 245/35 ZR 20 (front) - 305/30 ZR 21 (rear). **WEIGHT:** 1,585 kg. **ON SALE:** 2021 - . **VALUE IN 2025:** 130,000 - 200,000 eur.

911 (992) DAKAR
(2023)

ENGINE: 6-cylinder boxer 3,0 - **480 HP**. **MAXIMUM TORQUE:** 570 Nm @ 5,000 rpm. **TOP SPEED:** 240 km/h. **ACCELERATION 0-100 KM/H:** 3.4 sec. **AVERAGE FUEL CONSUMPTION:** 11.3 l/100 km. **DIMENSIONS (length/width/height):** 4.53 x 1.86 x 1.33 m. **WHEELBASE:** 2.45 m. **TYRES:** 245/45 ZR 19 (front) - 295/40 ZR 20 (rear). **WEIGHT:** 1,680 kg. **ON SALE:** 2023 - . **VALUE IN 2025:** 250,000 - 330,000 eur.

911 [992] TURBO
[2021]

ENGINE: 6-cylinder boxer 3,8 - **580 HP**. **MAXIMUM TORQUE:** 750 Nm @ 4,500 rpm. **TOP SPEED:** 320 km/h. **ACCELERATION 0-100 KM/H:** 2.8 sec. **AVERAGE FUEL CONSUMPTION:** 12.0 l/100 km. **DIMENSIONS (length/width/height):** 4.53 x 1.90 x 1.30 m. **WHEELBASE:** 2.45 m. **TYRES:** 255/35 ZR 20 (front) - 315/30 ZR 21 (rear). **WEIGHT:** 1,715 kg. **ON SALE:** 2021 - . **VALUE IN 2025:** 110,000 - 220,000 eur.

153

911 (992) TURBO S
(2021)

ENGINE: 6-cylinder boxer 3,8 - 650 HP. **MAXIMUM TORQUE:** 800 Nm @ 4,000 rpm. **TOP SPEED:** 330 km/h. **ACCELERATION 0-100 KM/H:** 2.7 sec. **AVERAGE FUEL CONSUMPTION:** 12.0 l/100 km. **DIMENSIONS (length/width/height):** 4.53 x 1.90 x 1.30 m. **WHEELBASE:** 2.45 m. **TYRES:** 255/35 ZR 20 (front) - 315/30 ZR 21 (rear). **WEIGHT:** 1,715 kg. **ON SALE:** 2021 - . **VALUE IN 2025:** 180,000 - 400,000 eur.

911 (992) GT3
(2022)

ENGINE: 6-cylinder boxer 4,0 - **510 HP**. **MAXIMUM TORQUE:** 470 Nm @ 6,100 rpm. **TOP SPEED:** 318 km/h. **ACCELERATION 0-100 KM/H:** 3.4 sec. **AVERAGE FUEL CONSUMPTION:** 12.9 l/100 km. **DIMENSIONS (length/width/height):** 4.57 x 1.85 x 1.28 m. **WHEELBASE:** 2.45 m. **TYRES:** 255/35 ZR 20 (front) - 315/30 ZR 21 (rear). **WEIGHT:** 1,493 kg. **ON SALE:** 2022 - . **VALUE IN 2025:** 170,000 - 290,000 eur.

911 (992) GT3 RS
(2023)

ENGINE: 6-cylinder boxer 4,0 - **525 HP**. **MAXIMUM TORQUE:** 465 Nm @ 6,300 rpm. **TOP SPEED:** 296 km/h. **ACCELERATION 0-100 KM/H:** 3.2 sec. **AVERAGE FUEL CONSUMPTION:** 13.4 l/100 km. **DIMENSIONS (length/width/height):** 4.57 x 1.90 x 1.32 m. **WHEELBASE:** 2.45 m. **TYRES:** 275/35 ZR 20 (front) - 335/30 ZR 21 (rear). **WEIGHT:** 1,525 kg. **ON SALE:** 2023 - . **VALUE IN 2025:** 290,000 - 550,000 eur.

159

911 (992) SPORT CLASSIC
(2023)

ENGINE: 6-cylinder boxer 3,8 - **550 HP**. **MAXIMUM TORQUE:** 600 Nm @ 6,000 rpm. **TOP SPEED:** 315 km/h. **ACCELERATION 0-100 KM/H:** 4.1 sec. **AVERAGE FUEL CONSUMPTION:** 12.6 l/100 km. **DIMENSIONS (length/width/height):** 4.53 x 1.90 x 1.30 m. **WHEELBASE:** 2.45 m. **TYRES:** 255/35 ZR 20 (front) - 315/30 ZR 21 (rear). **WEIGHT:** 1,645 kg. **ON SALE:** 2023 - . **VALUE IN 2025:** 300,000 - 480,000 eur.

911 (992) SPORT S/T
(2023)

ENGINE: 6-cylinder boxer 4,0 - **525 HP**. **MAXIMUM TORQUE:** 465 Nm @ -- rpm. **TOP SPEED:** 300 km/h. **ACCELERATION 0-100 KM/H:** 3.7 sec. **AVERAGE FUEL CONSUMPTION:** 13.8 l/100 km. **DIMENSIONS (length/width/height):** 4.57 x 1.85 x 1.28 m. **WHEELBASE:** 2.45 m. **TYRES:** 255/35 ZR 20 (front) - 315/30 ZR 21 (rear). **WEIGHT:** 1,455 kg. **ON SALE:** 2023 - . VALUE IN 2025: 400,000 - 550,000 eur.

60 YEARS OF HISTORY IN PICTURES

THANK YOU VERY MUCH!

I really appreciate the time you have taken to read this book.
It's an honour for me to enjoy this passion with
you and I would love to read your impressions on
Amazon about this book.
**Your ★★★★★ would be a great help
to continue this collection!**

We would all like to know what you thought of it
**"PORSCHE 911:
60 YEARS OF HISTORY IN PICTURES"!**

To leave your review on Amazon:

1.- Open your mobile phone camera.
2.- Focus your mobile phone on to the QR code.
3.- It will take you to the page where you can
leave your review.

If you want to contribute any ideas or make any comments
about the content of this book you can write to me at
inyeccionmultipunto.books@gmail.com

Made in the USA
Las Vegas, NV
13 December 2024